ULTIMATE STICKER BOOK TO COLOR

CARTOON NETWORK™

SCOOBY-DOO

LET'S STICK TOGETHER

® **Dalmatian Press, LLC, 2005. All rights reserved. Printed in Malaysia**
The DALMATIAN PRESS name and logo are trademarks of Dalmatian Press, LLC, Franklin, Tennessee 37067.
No part of this book may be reproduced or copied in any form without written permission from the copyright owner.

Dalmatian Press

13835 Scooby-Doo: Let's Stick Together
05 06 07 JPP 07 10 9 8 7 6 5 4 3 2 1

The Ghost of Hyde!

Escaped!

"Here you go—three liverwurst and onion sandwiches, a la mode."

"Come on, Scooby, time to go!"

Ride the waves

TM & © Hanna-Barbera.

"I have the chills, Scooby.
Fetch the blanket so we can bundle up."

Dalmatian Press

"Excuse re... RIIIPE!"

"Jinkies! Did you get a look at his face?
That's the creepy jewel thief, the Ghost of Mr. Hyde."
"Come on, let's follow him, gang."

"It's like a mad scientist's laboratory.
It must belong to the Ghost of Hyde."
"Zoinks! Someone's coming!"

"Like, what's with you, Scooby-Doo?!"

"Boy, like are we glad you didn't
turn out to be the ghost, Dr. Jekyll."
"I'm not so sure I'm not the ghost.
Look what I found in my pocket!"

"I was testing my new vitamin formula when I became dizzy.
The next thing I knew, my housekeeper, Helga, was waking
me up and I had the jewels in my pocket."

"We better split up and search for this ghost.
Watch out, gang!"

"Freddy said to search the place from top to bottom."

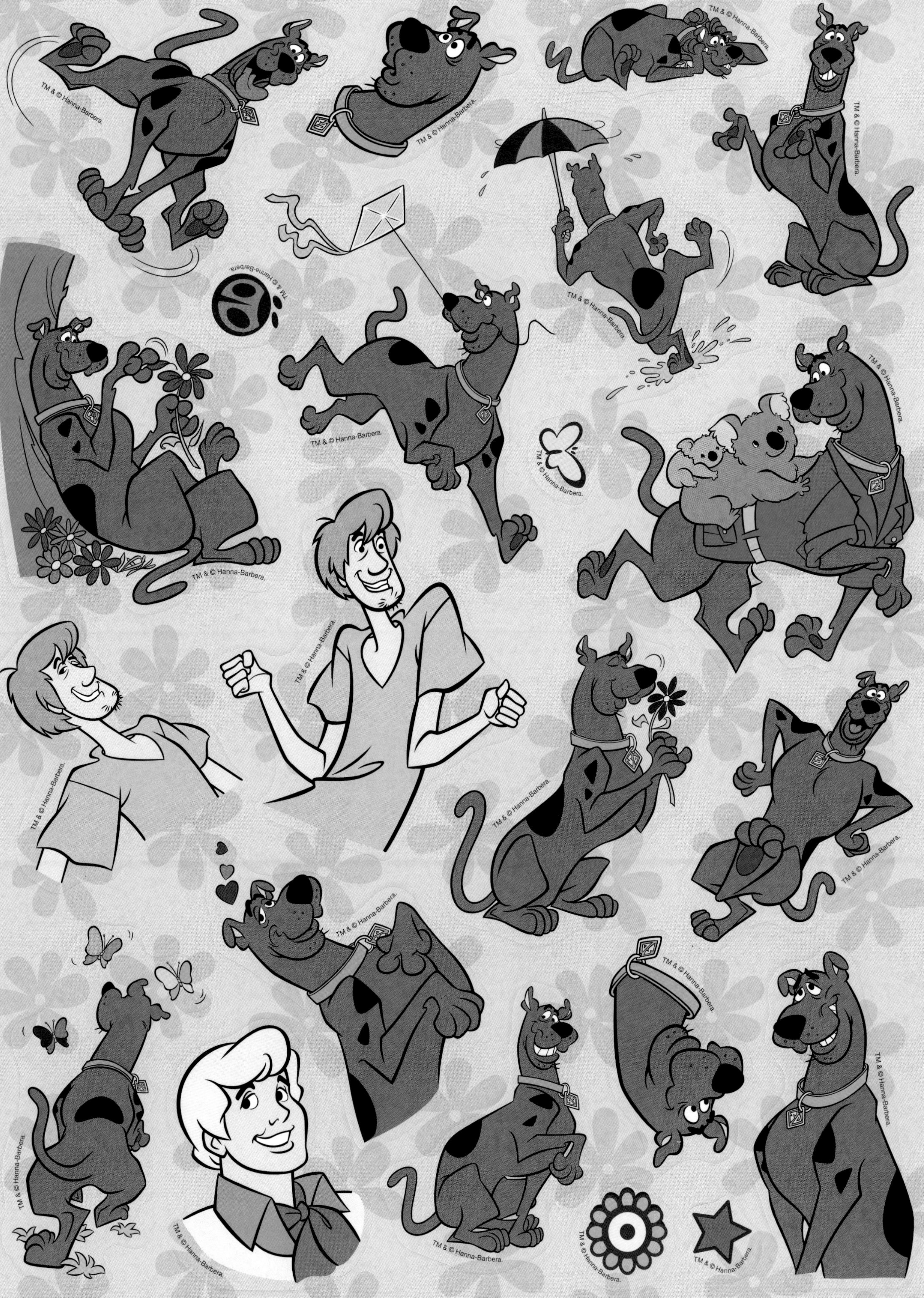
TM & © Hanna-Barbera.

13835 SD Ultimate Sticker BTC - Let's Stick Together

13835 SD Ultimate Sticker BTC - Let's Stick Together

SCOOBY-DOO

SCOOBY-DOO

TM & © Hanna-Barbera.

SD

TM & © Hanna-Barbera.

ACE

TM & © Hanna-Barbera.

"Maybe one of these books will give us a clue, Scooby-Doo."

"Zoinks! We hit the jackpot!"

"I sure hope Shaggy and Scooby are having
better luck than we are."
"Wait, I think I've found a clue.
It looks like someone was in a hurry to burn something."

"Hmm, so Helga the housekeeper used to be
a famous trapeze artist. I wonder…"

"I have a hunch we'll find more clues in Helga's room!"

"You're right, Velma.
Look! Face paint, vitamin pills and suction cups!"

"What would a famous circus performer
want with suction cups?"

"There you guys are, and just in time!
The Ghost of Hyde is a 24-karat phony."

"Now it's our turn to scare the hide out of Hyde.
Scooby and Shaggy can be the bait for our trap!"

"Ruh-roh!"
"How about a Scooby Snack? With ketchup and horseradish?"

"R'okay!"

"For he's an ugly masked fellow, that nobody can deny."

"The plan's working, Scoob!"

"Got 'im!"

13835 SD Ultimate Sticker BTC - Let's Stick Together

Scooby-Doo

13835 SD Ultimate Sticker BTC - Let's Stick Together

scooby-doo
**i love
you**
TM & © Hanna-Barbera.

Scooby-Doo
TM & © Hanna-Barbera.

SCOOBY-DOO

TM & © Hanna-Barbera.

Shaggy
TM & © Hanna-Barbera.

Scooby-Doo

Fred

"When Dr. Jekyll's crazy experiments failed,
he decided to turn to a life of crime.
His climbing act was only an attempt to frame Helga."
"Great work, gang!"

Daphne Blake & Fred Jones

Velma Dinkley & Norville "Shaggy" Rogers

Scooby-Doo and the gang attend a charity fashion show.
The event's donations will help build a
new pet orphanage for the town.

"This town doesn't need a pet orphanage,"
Dog Catcher Taggert tells the Mayor.
"There are too many animals! They'll get out and run wild!"

Daphne and Velma love fashion shows.
They both dream of modeling fabulous dresses!

Suddenly, the Fashion Phantom attacks! "Ha ha ha ha ha ha!"

"It's terrible!" cries the show's organizer.
"The dresses were stolen! The fashion show is ruined!"

"Don't worry," says Fred. "We'll solve this mystery!"

"You know, we can still have dresses for the fashion show,"
suggests Daphne. "Help us look for fabrics in these old boxes."

"We'll make new fashions from these items," Velma and Daphne
explain, "and decorate them with stencils and markers!"

The boys look for clues in the basement until...

"Ha ha ha ha ha! The Fashion Phantom has you!"

Scooby-Doo Sports
MYSTERY INC.

POW!

SCOOBY-DOO SPORTS

CHAMP

TOUCHDOWN

SCOOBY-DOO TOUCHDOWN

KNOCKOUT

Dalmatian Press

13835 SD Ultimate Sticker BTC - Let's Stick Together

Daphne

The guys beat a noisy retreat through the music room.

"Whew! That was a close one, guys!"

**"Listen, guys, we can play the Fashion Phantom's game.
I've got a plan!"**

"Okay, you two, I'll give you each an armload of Scooby Snacks," promises Fred, "if you pretend to be his long-lost brothers."

"Like, hey, big brother! Long time no see." Scooby-Doo and Shaggy distract the Phantom, while Fred readies the trap.

"Zoinks! Run, Scoob!
Like, that creepy Phantom isn't too fond of relatives!"

"Freeze, Phantom! The jig is up! This is the police!"

Fred's trick works!
The unmasked Fashion Phantom is Dog Catcher Taggert!

The boys find the stolen dresses! As the real police
take Taggert away, he grumbles, "Meddling kids!"

"We didn't need those dresses after all.
Daphne and Velma showed us how to make new fashions!"

**Daphne and Velma join the show
and model the dresses recovered by the boys.**

Even Scooby-Doo gets in on the fashion action!

**The charity fashion show is a huge success!
Enough money is raised to open a pet orphanage...**

...and Scooby and Shaggy each get armloads
of Scooby Snacks! Now, that's good taste!